T0366096

Brenda Robinson & Harley Robinson

WRITING FOR THE WORLD OF WORK

"Writing right—a clear, concise, complete, correct and courteous approach to good business writing"

Order this book online at **www.trafford.com**
or email orders@trafford.com

Most Trafford titles are also available at major online book retailers.

Printed in the United States of America.

ISBN: 978-1-4669-1312-7 (sc)
ISBN: 978-1-4669-1317-2 (e)

Trafford rev. 03/08/2012

 www.trafford.com

North America & International
toll-free: 1 888 232 4444 (USA & Canada)
phone: 250 383 6864 • fax: 812 355 4082

CONTENTS

Introduction

Writing for the World of Work

Writing for the world of work is a communication skill as much as a writing skill. Writing at work today is our way of communicating—we email more than we converse. Our writing now "speaks" for us. Technology has not decreased the need for effective writing skills at work. Indeed, there may actually be an increased demand for good writers as we embrace the world of emails, electronic reporting, instant messaging and. . .

We have a new kind of reader today. Readers used to expect to have to read, reread, interpret, sort and select as a part of the process. They expected to have to work hard to get the information.

Today's reader only wants to read once, understand at the first reading and be able to make a decision. In fact, it is preferable to be able to simply skim and easily find the information that is needed.

Not only has the reader changed, the readers expectations have also changed. I call it being "CSI'd." The TV show CSI follows a particular format. They show you the crime right up front and the rest of the story is about understanding the crime. When we're writing for work we need to keep in mind that people want the important stuff first and then the explanation.

As the pace of work continues to increase, people have less time to compose, create, review and study the written information at work. They want to write quickly, clearly and directly and they want to get results! The reader wants to read once, understand the first reading and take the action required! Everybody wants to complete the process with ease, speed and accuracy. In order to do this, writers need to write for readers. Our training has not always been to write for the reader to understand. In fact, more often than not, a writer wanted to impress the reader.

Do you remember the writing you did in school? Did you try to use bigger words? Did you try hard to sound more impressive by using your thesaurus? Did anybody ever tell you that simple sentences were for simple people? Did you try to use longer, more compound and complex sentences? Did you worry about how your writing flowed? Did you work hard to provide unity and coherence?

All of these ideas were excellent guidelines for writing essays, papers, book reports and academic documents. But, do they work when we are writing for the world of work? The key element that sets the world of work apart is the need for clear communication. In our workplaces, we do not need to be impressed as much as we need to understand.

Indeed, when we write for work it is far more important to express the information than impress the reader. Expressing information often means being clear, concise, complete, correct and courteous. Readers read and understand best the writing that is short, simple and specific. This often means using the thesaurus in reverse—looking up short, simple words to replace long, unfamiliar ones. It means short sentences, short paragraphs, more point form and ease of reading.

Then, we need also to be aware that the world of work is full of busy people. They need the information in direct ways that generate action instead of reaction. When we offend or upset our reader with negativity, doubt, threats or lack of understanding, we will not get the results we want. Although objectivity is still important, it must be balanced with the human factor. Messages must be given in positive, considerate ways. We have a new reader in the world of work who reads the tone as well as the message. Even negative messages need to be presented in positive ways. We must focus our writing in such a way that it appeals to the reader. The goal of writing at work is to achieve understanding, shared information and action.

We are faced with breaking old habits in our written communication. Our writing must be up to date, interesting, informative and reader oriented. This is the challenge of "Writing for the World of Work."

Chapter 1

A Quick Review of Basic Writing

Why the English language is so hard to learn. . .

We know the word is box, and the plural is boxes
But the plural of ox is oxen not oxes

There is a single mouse and a nest full of mice
Yet the plural of house is houses not hice

We can see one man and two are called men
Yet the plural of pan is never called pen

One fowl is a goose, a gaggle are geese
Yet the family of moose is never called meese

We say the word tooth and the plural is teeth
Yet the plural of booth is never called beeth

The masculine pronouns are he his and him
So why aren't the feminines she, shes and shim?

Writing for the World of Work requires accuracy and correctness in our use of language. It is almost impossible to look at all the rules of the English language. However, there are a few quick rules which help us review and update our writing.

Here are some hints and tips to help you write with confidence and clarity. It is not always necessary to know all of the rules as long as you can recognize the mistake and change the writing to get rid of the error. The two best ways to check for correct use of the written language are:

> Read your writing out loud.
> Ask somebody else to read it for you or to you.

We often hear a mistake that we wouldn't be able to see. Give your writing the auditory test!

What are you looking for as you work to achieve accuracy and correctness? Here are some of the common considerations for writing at work.

1. Grammar

- Have I used direct statements?

- Do my verbs agree with my subjects?

  Example:
  I am
  They are
  He is

- Do I have consistent verb tenses in my writing?

Example:
Past
Present
Future

- Have I achieved parallelism?

Example:
She was sitting at her desk and worked on her computer

She was sitting at her desk and working on her computer

2. Spelling

- Have I used words which are familiar to me and my reader? Many spelling mistakes can be avoided by using words we know well and use often.

- Have I used short words instead of long words—they are easier to spell.

    Example:
    Use—instead of utilize
    End—instead of termination

- Have I used spell check? Some words require extra scrutiny. Here is a list of common misspelled words that your spell check won't catch:

Here	Hear
Their	There
Weather	Whether
Through	Threw

Roll	Role
Poll	Pole

Add to your list and give these words special attention.

- Have I used Canadian spelling? Generally speaking, the Canadian spelling is the longer one:

    Example: Neighbour   (Canadian)   Neighbor (American)

    Although there is an increase in acceptance in both spellings, we still encourage Canadian usage.

Here are the most frequently asked questions about grammar

✓ When to use who and when to use whom?

Who is the subject or doer of the action

Whom is the object or reciever of the action.

Whom must follow a verb or a preposition (To, From, For or About)

Example:

Who wants to drive? (who is the subject, wants is the action/verb)

The report asks whom is responsible? (Whom is the reciever of the action asks)

Do you see how awkward whom sounds? In writing for the world of work, we recommend avoiding the word whom.

✓ When to use it's and when to use its?

It's is a contraction and only stands for it is.

Everything else is its.

Example:

It's time to leave.

The dog is wagging its tail.

Its is the only word that shows possession without an apostrophe. There is no such word as its'.

✓ When to use we're, were and where

Example:

We're the contraction for we are. (We're looking after the books)

Were is a verb. (The books were in the library.)

Where is a location. (Where is the library?)

✓ When to use he're, hear, and here.

Example:

He're is the contraction of here are. (He're are the reports.)

Hear is the action of hearing. (Did you hear about the report?)

Here is a location. (Could you bring the report here?)

✓ When to use they're, their and there.

Example:

They're is the contraction for they are. (They're leaving their suitcases.)

Their is possession. (Their suitcases were left behind.)

There is location. (Their suitcases are over there.)

✓ When to use seen and when to use scene.

Example:

Seen is a verb. (She has already seen her manager.)

Scene is a noun. (He is in one scene in the play or she left the scene of the accident.)

✓ When to use sight, site and cite.

Example:

Sight is a noun relating to visual ability. (She has good sight.)

Site is a location. (We are going to the construction site.)

Cite is a verb meaning referring to or pointing to. (Please cite the bylaw you are using.)

✓ When to use fowl and when to use foul.

Example:

Fowl is a noun meaning a feathered bird. (How many fowl on your farm?)

Foul is an adjective meaning not correct or inappropriate. (He hit a foul ball or it was a foul odour.)

✓ When to use read, reed, or reid.

Example:

Read is a verb (Did you read the book?)

Reed is a part of a musical instrument (the clarinet has reed) Reed is also a part of a plant (the fern has a reed.)

Reid is just a name.

✓ When to use who's and whose.

Example:

Who's is a contraction for who is. (Who's coming in this car?)

Whose indicates possession. (Whose car is it?)

Always remember—some words need an extra look. <u>Read</u> before you <u>send.</u>

3. Punctuation

- Have I used punctuation to increase clarity and understanding?

- Did I remember the question marks?

- Shorter sentences create less need for punctuation.

- Have I eliminated semi-colons (;) from my writing—the semi colon confuses the reader. It also makes a long sentence.

- Have I minimized the use of the dash?

- Have I used open punctuation in my point form writing? There is no "end of point" punctuation required.

- Did I use the colon (:) to indicate a list of points or items?

Once again, reading your writing out loud is a good measure of the appropriateness of your punctuation. Punctuation should provide natural pauses. In fact, you may give your writing the "breathing" test. Take a breath with every form of punctuation. Can you continue reading with ease? Are you breathless or are you breathing rapidly? Reading should not exhaust the reader.

4. Sentences

Sentence structure may be your most powerful tool for effective writing. Sentences are the way we express our ideas and tie them together to make sense for the reader. The best sentences are those which read quickly, easily and with clarity. Ask yourself the following questions about your use of sentences as you write:

- Are my sentences short and to the point?

- Have I used sentence variety—questions, exclamations?

- Are most of my sentences simple sentences? Compound/complex sentences are difficult to read and understand.

- Does each sentence contain one piece of key information?

- Have I checked the length of my sentences? (17 words at the most)

- Have I used point form whenever possible?

- Have I limited the use of passive sentences and replaced them with active sentences?

Example:

Passive   The report was written by the assistant manager.

Active   The assistant manager wrote the report.

5. Paragraphs

This was the scary part of writing for many students. Teachers always talked about paragraph development in a way that made it sound challenging and difficult. Actually a paragraph is just a brief discussion of an idea. Paragraphs break the reading into manageable chunks for the reader. Review your paragraphs by asking yourself the following questions:

- Are my paragraphs easy to read and follow?

- Did I limit my paragraphs to five or six sentences?

- Did I use transition words to tie my paragraph together?

Example:

In addition . . .   However . . .

Further to . . .   Therefore . . .

6. Numbers, symbols, abbreviations and acronyms.

Readers slow down when they read numbers, symbols and abbreviations. We must be certain that our numbers, symbols and abbreviations are clear and easy to understand. Indeed, they should facilitate the ease of reading and understanding. Here are some helpful tips for using numbers, symbols and abbreviations:

- When using numbers under ten, write the numbers in a word format

Example: one, two

- When you use two numbers together, write out one of them in word format.

Example: fourteen 20 cm boards

- When you use an abbreviation or acronym it is important to clearly define it at the first use.

Example: PW—Public Works

PAO—Personnel Administration Office

- Use consistent acronyms and abbreviations throughout your writing.

- Limit the use of symbols to the ones that are easily recognized and familiar to the reader. Some of the commonly used symbols include

Example: $-dollars

#-number

@-at

Some symbols to avoid include:

i.e (for example)

vs (instead of)

Always ask yourself if the reader will clearly understand the abbreviation, acronym or symbol you have used. They should not have to look it up, check back or ask for a definition. Remember, the reader wants to read once, understand at the first reading, and take the action required. Make it easy for the reader.

Chapter 2

Writing for the Reader—Readability

In one of my very first jobs I had the opportunity to do some huge learning about business writing. I was a strong academic student. I particularly took pride in my writing skills. My major course of study was Shakespearean literature. I was the typical university English graduate.

I worked for a large retail organization. I was hired into a management training program. After about three months, I was called into the CEO's office. "I understand you have a degree in English," he said, as soon as I arrived in his office. "I need somebody to study the feasibility of this new cash register system and write a report with recommendations."

I readily agreed. Writing was my strength. This was the task for me! I left his office full of confidence—maybe even a little arrogance.

I was given two weeks to complete the research and write the report. I began immediately. I researched with a vengeance! I read all available documentation. I interviewed people who were currently using the system. I went directly to the manufacturer. I collected data and evidence to support my work. Finally, I wrote the report. It was a thing of beauty! It was 120 pages including a 26 page appendix. It was beautifully formatted and Cerlox bound with a cardboard cover.

I took it to my boss with pride and trepidation. I handed it over as if it were a sacred possession. He picked it up and looked at the cover. He then opened it and flipped through it for about ten seconds. At this point he looked up at me and said, "Can you give it to me on one page?"

I was shocked and appalled. How could I possibly give him all of my research and documentation in one page? This was a huge report! There were endless details to recount. My cost comparison charts alone took 3 pages. What kind of person was I working for? Didn't he understand the need for clarity and accuracy in reporting? I couldn't possibly say it all on one page!

I left his office annoyed, frustrated, confused and worried. I talked to all my co-workers about my conundrum. They seemed to think I was exaggerating. Generally, they agreed that if he wanted one page, I should give him one page.

What was I going to do? I sat down with my report and wrote a one page summary. I made my recommendations. I gave five key statements to support my recommendations. I included the cost of the system, the cost of installation as well as the cost savings over the first year and beyond. I attached the one page summary to the front of my 120 page report. I was not giving up that easily on my comprehensive document.

I returned to my boss's office and handed him my report again, with the summary attached. He read the summary. He never looked at the rest of my report. Instead, he looked at me and said, "Are you sure of this?" I replied, "Yes." He said, "Well then, we'll go ahead with your recommendations." I don't know if he ever read the rest of the report.

Months later, I asked him about it. He told me that he trusted me to do good research. He believed that the supporting data was in the report. All he needed was the recommendations.

What did I learn? We have to write for our reader. Our reader wants the key information right up front. The first page is the most important page. Quality is more important than quantity.

People read 90% of page 1, 80% of page 2 and 50% of page 3. If you are lucky after that they are reading 10% of each page. What does that tell us about the order of information? Get the important information up front!

This challenges our thinking about how to organize our information. All of our academic teaching told us to begin with an introduction and to end with a conclusion. We now know that the reader is looking for the conclusion first.

A letter, memo, email or report is only successful when it has been read and understood. Readability is the rate with which your reader can read and understand your writing.

Our writing instruction was almost always from the writer's point of view. How about the reader? Readability is the key to the success of your report or letter.

We have to be careful in all of our writing to understand the relationship between these two elements for the reader. Our responsibility as a writer is to write a report, a memo, a letter or an email to meet the following criteria:

- The reader will only have to read it once

- The reader will understand at the first reading

- The reader will not have to question the content

- The reader will be able to refer back to the document with ease

- The reader will be able to discuss what has been written

Most readers read best at the grade 7, 8 or 9 levels. Although education is one of the factors, it is certainly not the only determining factor in reading level. As soon as we leave the academic setting, our reading level begins to drop off. Why? Because most of our reading on a daily basis is not academic reading.

Newspapers, magazines and leisure reading materials are written at levels varying form Grade 4 to Grade 10. This often makes up the majority of our reading. When we read daily at this level, our academic ability to read and understand at higher levels soon decreases.

Furthermore, the reasons for reading and the approach to reading change when we leave the academic world. On the job, we have no inclination to study and memorize what we read. When we approach an email, letter, memo or report, we want to read and understand—at the first reading.

What can you do as a writer to ensure the most appropriate readability level for your reader? You would probably be well advised to aim at Grade 7 or 8 with slight adjustments for specific readers. No reader will be offended by this level and it is a good safe level to ensure understanding.

There are five components of the readability factor in writing for work.

On the following pages are some suggestions for effectively looking after the readability level in your writing.

Words:

- Use simple words

- Use short words

- Use specific words

- Avoid jargon words

- Try to avoid words with more than 3 syllables

- Avoid words with local meaning only

- Provide definition of technical terms

- Avoid slang and "fad" words

- Avoid outdated words

Word choice must be directed by a concern for the reader. Readers read best when words contain fewer than three syllables. Words should also be chosen to speak to the reader. The reader wants to read as if they are in conversation with the writer.

In academic writing we use an inflated language designed to meet quantity goals not quality goals. In some organizations we also develop an inflated language.

Example:

- Nothing ever ends—it terminates

- Nothing gets used—it gets utilized

- Things aren't started—they are initiated or implemented

- We don't work together—we develop partnerships.

Not only do people not want to read this style, they do not remember it even if they do in fact read it. There is an old saying that I use to illustrate this idea:

Early to bed, early to rise makes a man healthy, wealthy and wise.

Would anyone remember it if it went like this:

Early to bed, early to rise makes a man opulent, sagacious and sonubulent.

When writing for work people have to want to read it and be able to understand it. At work we arrive and sit down, open our email and find that we have 42 new email messages. What does that tell us about the amount of time and energy we have to both read and understand?

There used to be two languages, (or at least two versions.) We spoke in one language and we wrote in another. We now know that they are coming closer together. We may not be quite ready for all out texting. However, we need to find a balance between old formal words and the new language that technology brings.

Phrases:

- Be as concise as possible

- Update phrases

- Avoid unnecessary padding

- Avoid double statements

- Use specific descriptions

- Use connecting transition phrases only when necessary

- Watch for overused phrases

Phrases are what gives us our ability to write in quantity vs. quality. We often choose to use phrases made up of four to five words, when one word would do.

Example:

We say "rectangular in shape" when simply saying "rectangle" would do in most cases.

We also sometimes say "begin to introduce" when simply saying "introduce" will most often work fine.

I have heard people say, "work on developing" in situations where simply using the word "developing" would have sufficed.

Phrases often just serve to make our writing longer and more formal. They take away from the conversational tone we are trying to achieve.

For Example:

If you were drowning you would never shout "It would be deeply appreciated if you would come to my assistance at this time."

Today we are drowning in the amount of information being sent and received. We need to find shorter ways to ask for help! In fact we need to find shorter ways to communicate for business.

Sentences:

- Keep sentences short

- Give one piece of information per sentence

- Use more simple sentences

- Try to keep sentences to 17 words (14 words for reading on the screen)

- Use punctuation to increase understanding

- Use point form when possible

Sentences are the way that people connect information. When a sentence is more than 14 - 17 words, the reader stops reading. The reader starts reading again at the beginning of the next sentence. If important information is contained in the end of a long sentence it can easily be missed.

Sentence variety is also an important element of writing for work. We have always written in a narrative, almost monotone way. We need to use more questions, exclamations and partial sentences. That's what conversations sound like!

Good sentences work to keep your reader interested.

Paragraphs:

- Keep only one idea per paragraph

- Try to keep paragraphs to 4 - 6 sentences

- Try to keep paragraphs to 80 - 100 words

- Connect paragraphs using transition words

- Use logical sequence for each paragraph

- Make a point in each paragraph

The secret to writing good paragraphs is to write shorter and fewer paragraphs.

It is still important for a paragraph to contain information related to one idea. However, it may take several paragraphs to fully expand on that idea.

Transition Words

Good paragraph writing includes the use of transition words and phrases to tie information together.

Examples:

- However. . .

- In addition. . .

- A second point. . .

These words help to keep the reader interested by connecting the writer's ideas or points together.

Pages:

- Make each page look inviting to read

- Provide a border around the page when appropriate

- Provide headings to divide material

- Organize each page with 4-6 paragraphs

- Ensure that each page provides the reader with 6 breaks

- Format each page to maintain 25% white space

A page of writing is often the first impression that the reader has of the writer. When the reader looks at a page and it looks easy to read, the motivation to read the entire page, is high. When the same reader first eyes a page of heavy narrative the motivation to read it is much, much lower.

The motivation to read the page depends on the level of appeal, which comes from:

- Short words

- Short sentences

- Short paragraphs

- Enough white space

Sometimes, our writing style gets in the way of our content.

I was involved once in the challenge of "writing up" the results of environmental research. The writers were researchers through and through. They had backgrounds in the sciences—biology, chemistry and environmental study.

A huge research project had been commissioned to determine the impact that a certain project was having on the environment. Indeed, the specific focus was the impact on large antlered animals and their breeding habits. Apparently there was concern that the presence of an overhead pipeline would interfere with the movements of these animals. Movement was considered important because "the chase" had always been a part of the breeding activities in question.

After four years of research and endless deliberation, the decision was made. The pipeline would be placed 11 feet off the ground. This would ensure clearance for all of the large antlered animals. The migration, the wandering and especially the breeding habits of these animals would be secure.

When the pipeline was in use and the weight increased, it moved up and down as the ground conditions changed with the seasons. Awareness of this grew and soon became a cry of alarm from environmentalists advocating in the region. What about the breeding habits of the large antlered animals? If the pipeline was now only 10' 2" in some place and it was required to be 11', what did this mean? The environmentalists were appalled.

It was back to the drawing board for the study. New parameters were set out. Researchers returned to the area and a whole new study was commissioned. This time, the researchers spent three years researching and three months writing the report. Everyone waited in anxious anticipation for the results.

The finished report looked like a National Geographic book. It was beautiful to behold! It had a bound hardcover and included pictures, graphs, charts, maps, and all on stunningly glossy colour pages. It was delivered with great ceremony to the pipeline company for review.

Forty minutes later it was returned to the research group by bicycle courier. Attached was a yellow sticky note which read:

"What about the breeding habits of the large antlered animals? Where is that information?

The researchers were furious! They said, "It's all in there—all they had to do was read." They even made comments about the pipeline folks not being able to read. They were defensive, frustrated and confused. They knew the information was in the report.

That is when I got a call. The researchers wanted to know if I could help them. "How do we get these people to read the report?" they asked. I agreed to take a look and see if I could help out.

When I received the report I was appalled. It was certainly beautiful and it contained some amazing pictures. It was 142 pages with a 26 page appendix. (We should always remember that the appendix of a report is like our own appendix—we can live without it!)

The first 17 pages were introduction. The introduction talked about the purpose and scope of the report. (Both were well known to the reader.) There were six pages devoted to expressions of appreciation. They thanked the providers of supplies, the local people who helped out, the camera suppliers, the providers of ATV's and transportation and on and on and on. They outlined the methods of research, (these were the same as the previous study.) They spent 17 pages giving the reader information they already had or weren't concerned about. This all happened because in the academic world where most researchers live, reports are written with:

- Introduction

- Discussion

- Conclusion

These researchers believed they were providing the foundations of a good report. They were writing from the writer's perspective. They forgot about the reader's perspective. What did the readers at the pipeline company want to see when they opened the report? Do we have to spend multi $$$ revamping, raising and securing this pipeline?

The reader in today's world is impatient and demanding. They want to see the information they need on the first page. They do not want to read, study and search for the key information.

We began to re-write the report. The research was accurate, convincing and influential. It just needed to be presented for the readers' purpose. Our re-write followed the "reader driven" order:

- Conclusion

- Justification

- Summary

On page one, we started with, "The breeding and migration habits of the large antlered animals are not impacted by. . ." We provided the four key findings.

On page two we started with the recommendations.

"There is no requirement to make changes or adjustments to the pipeline." "The breeding and migration habits of the large antlered animals are not affected by. . ."

Pages 3 to 23 summarized the research, (mostly in point form.) Page 24 contained a summary of the conclusions and recommendations. When a chart or graph was required we placed it in the body of the report where it was referred to. We did include 14 of the pictures in the appendix. They were indeed interesting and beautiful.

What did we leave out? We left out additional research. There was information on the coyote cycles. There was research about an endangered hawk in the area. There was research done on water quality and weather patterns. There was information about the migrating geese and the changes in food supply for all birds in the area. Interesting indeed, but not relevant to this reader.

The result was a 24 page report with a 14 page appendix. We used a cerlox binder with a clean cover and sent it off to the pipeline company. They replied 15 minutes later with a "Thank-You," Of course they were happy with the report. They knew immediately that no action was required. They did not need to spend a fortune to recover.

One of the researchers said he felt guilty about providing such a small report for such a long and extensive study. Once again we see the quantity versus quality measure for writing success. Another researcher said, "You left out so much valuable information!" The question is—who is that information valuable to? Information must have value for the reader. There may be other reports where that information will fit.

The data, the observations and the analysis all supported the conclusions and recommendations. On a brighter note, the researchers reported that a pipeline suspended at 10 feet in this area was never going to be a barrier for a large antlered male pursuing a female in breeding season. Indeed, if necessary the male would crawl on his knees to reach the female of his quest. The folks at the pipeline company appreciated the humour of this observation.

The learning? Write for the reader. Address the readers' needs. Understand the difference between academic writing and business writing. Get to the point, the reader wants and needs it. Update your formats and style. Make your writing reader friendly.

Chapter 3

Updating our Writing

A friend of mine applied for a job with a large bureaucracy. Two weeks later he got the "letter." It started out, "We regret to inform you. . ." He read the opening and tossed the letter aside. In great frustration he said, "They probably had the person picked before they posted it." "Besides, it's not what you know, it's who you know." He ripped the letter up and stuffed it in the garbage.

Three weeks later, we were at a wine and cheese party when someone asked my friend why he missed the interview. Confused, he replied "I never had an interview—I was turned down for the job." We found a copy of the letter. The first line was as he remembered: "We regret to inform you that you were unsuccessful in your application for the Sales and Service position."

The second line was not what he had expected at all. It said: "However, we have a similar opening, with emphasis on public relations and specialized marketing. We believe you would be an excellent fit. Could you come for an interview on Friday, February 4, 2011 at 3:00 pm?"

Some may say he should have read the whole letter. How about the responsibility the writer has to keep the reader reading?

Business writing has not been updated even though all of the technology around writing has. When we tried to update, we just put our old templates into new technology. Updating often meant changing names, dates, formats etc. . . But we never changed the style. When people were asked to draft a document or template, they simply went into the files and copied what had been done before.

Business writing has always been influenced by statements or attitudes like:

- That's the way we have always done it

- That's the way I was trained to do it

- I had a teacher / professor who told us. . .

Indeed, business writing has always been a combination of legal and academic writing. That's why it's so formal and heavy and that's where our updating needs to begin.

Out of Date Courtesies

In an era where terms of intimacy may constitute grounds for workplace harassment we may want to update the salutations in our business writing.

Think of it like this, you wouldn't phone a client or customer and say, *"Dear Frank"* or *"Dear Shirley."* Nor would you open a business meeting with, *"To whom it may concern."* People like to be addressed by name and generally by first name.

In this era a business writer needs to be cautious about terms of address. Words like, Mr, Ms, Mrs. Miss may be stereotypical and may even offend the reader before you even begin to write to them. First Name, First and Last Name, or Initials with the Last Name are the most appropriate way to address people today.

It is particularly important to avoid multiple addresses such as:

- Dear Sirs / Mesdames

- Ladies and Gentlemen

- Dear Sir / Madam

- Dear Sirs

It is also important to stay away from generic addresses such as:

- Dear Head of Household

- Dear Homeowner

- Dear Taxpayer

- Dear Resident

- Dear Community Member

The best salutations (openings) look like this:

- Brenda Robinson:

- B. Robinson:

- Brenda:

Or

- Harley Robinson:

- H. Robinson:

- Harley:

The colon following the name indicates a business letter.

It is equally important to update the endings of our business communications. In business emails for example, the end salutation has essentially been replaced by a block of contact information. Old formal complimentary closes no longer have meaning because they come out of an era where only personal and legal letters were written. We need to update by replacing closings such as:

- Yours truly,

- Yours very truly,

- Your Humble and Obedient Servant,

- Yours Respectfully,

- Respectfully Yours,

- Yours Sincerely,

The word yours is an intimacy and does not belong in writing for work.

Appropriate closings include:

- Sincerely,

- Cheers,

- Take Care,

- Regards,

- Best Regards,

- Thank You,

Some writers choose to eliminate the complimentary close.

You will find that most of the updating is actually in the openings and closings in business communication. Look carefully at your opening and closing lines. Do they sound like something you would say in conversation?

How many times have you said in conversation, *"Kindly Advise. . ."*

Or for that matter, how often do you run into someone in the hall and say, *"We wish to acknowledge . . ."*

Or, have you ever left a meeting and said on your way out, *"Hoping to hear from you soon."*

The answer would be, *"go on hoping—maybe you will, maybe you won't."*

We tend to use closings which are not meaningful such as:

> *"If you have any problems or difficulties, please don't hesitate to contact me."*

Are you trying to encourage them to come up with a problem?

> *"Please feel free to contact me for additional information."*

Is there actually additional information and if so, why didn't you give it to them in the first place? Besides, what does *feel free* really mean?

The key to updating is to read your writing aloud. Does it sound like something you would actually say? How often do you "speak" these common business terms?

- We Regret to Inform. . .

- Enclosed Please Find. . .

- Herewith Enclosed. . .

- We Wish to Inform. . .

- We Beg To Acknowledge. . .

- Kindly Respond. . .

- It Behoves Me To Say. . .

- It Gives Me Great Pleasure. . .

Get right to the point.

- Thank you for applying. . .

- Here is your cheque for $800 . . .

- Your meeting is confirmed for . . .

- Will you call us at _____ by Thursday?

- Thanks again for keeping us up to date. . .

- Good news!

These updates, need to be combined with updating our formatting. Moving away from old fashioned formats such as complete block will provide an updated look in your business communications.

Here are some examples of updating:

Example 1:

We beg to advise that your project has been delayed due to inadvertent climatic conditions.

It would be deeply appreciated if you would advise us of any changes prior to commencement of said project.

Please allow us to express our appreciation for your continued patience with the project initiation.

Hoping to hear from you soon, I remain.

Yours Very Truly,

Bob Hoskins

Rewrite:

It is important for you to know that your project is delayed due to poor weather.

Will you let us know of any changes before the project starts?

Thanks for being patient. Will you call us to confirm the new start date?

Bob Hoskins

Example 2:

Please find enclosed your cheque calculated to a total of $144.87.

Please acknowledge receipt of the above stated payment at your earliest convenience. We look forward to your reply and thank-you in advance.

Rewrite:

Here is your cheque for $144.87. Will you confirm that you received the cheque?

Thank-you.

Chapter 4

Write for the Reader—Tone and Approach

The "You" Attitude

Writing for the reader includes a "You" attitude. The "You" attitude can be defined as the writer's ability to write for the reader. When we write using the "You" attitude we talk first and most often about the reader. In typical business writing we often begin with an I, we, our or the name of the company or organization. This leaves the reading wondering, *what's in it for them?* We say the reader is tuned in to WIIFM, *(What's in it for me?)*

There are 5 techniques that bring the "You" attitude into your business communication:

1. Use questions to emphasize the reader.

> For Example:

> *We would like to invite you to chair our meeting on March 31.*

Should be written like this:

Will you chair our meeting on March 31?

2. **Always try to refer to the reader before referring to you or your department / workplace.**

For Example:

We are writing to inform you that your report will be ready on February 1.

Should be written like this:

Your report will be ready on February 1.

3. **Personalize your business writing, by using the reader's name in the context of the message. Always use and spell names correctly.**

For Example:

Thank you Sara, for working with us this past weekend.

Or like this:

Emily, were you able to process the invoice for the supplies?

Remember, the names must be spelled correctly and not overused. One or two references are enough.

4. **Count the number of (I / We) messages as compared to the number of (You / Your) messages. The (You / Your) messages should outnumber the (I / We) messages.**

You / Your	I / We
You	I
Your	We
Yours	Me
"The Person's Name"	My
	Mine
	Our
	Ours
	Us
	On Behalf Of

For Example:

We are writing to invite you to our spring gala.

Here the writer uses an I / We choice twice. While using You / Your only once.

Should be written like this:

Do you have time in your schedule to come to our spring gala.

In this example the (I / We) choices are outnumbered by the (You / Your) choices.

5. **Always try to close your correspondence emphasizing the reader and his/her concerns.**

For Example:

Thank you for your support.

Instead of:

I wish to express my appreciation for your support.

Here are some examples of the power of the "You" attitude:

Example 1:

I am writing to ask you to send 14 copies of your annual report. I will be distributing these to our executive members to help them update for our upcoming meeting.

I would appreciate receiving these by April 1, 2010.

Rewrite:

Will you send 14 copies of your annual report? Your report will help our executive members understand your organization better. It will also help them be better prepared to meet with your team on May 1, 2010.

Could you send them by April 1, 2010 for distribution at our April 5 staff meeting? Thank you for your help.

Example 2:

We require a guest speaker for our conference on April 21. I would like to invite you to share your experience with us. We are planning a full day conference and would like you to be our opening speaker.

Please let me know at your earliest convenience whether or not you can join us.

Rewrite:

Will you join us to share your expertise at our conference on April 21? Could you be our opening speaker to start off a full day event?

Your knowledge and expertise combined with your dynamic presentation style will be the perfect "kick off" for the conference.

Will you confirm your participation by email by April 1? Thank you.

Positive Tone:

Most of us have very little difficulty writing with a positive message. In fact, most of us look forward to a letter of congratulations or even a "thank you" note. But when we have to say "we can't" or "we didn't" or "I'm sorry", it's often a struggle to choose the right word in the right way.

A positive tone is required even when the message is negative. Remember, a letter is a public relations agent for you and your organization. You may have to say "no", but you don't want to leave a negative image with your reader.

Is it possible to say "no" in a positive way? Yes! What does it take? It takes very careful word choice, planning and the ability to emphasize what can be done instead of what can't be done.

Have you ever had the experience of receiving a letter that starts out, We regret to inform you. . .?" Did you have to read the rest of the letter? Words like, regret, unfortunately and sorry serve to inform the reader that the content of the message is negative. Most readers do not want to read a negative message. They often stop reading at that point. Even if there is something positive or encouraging in the rest of the message they may not get it.

The new ratio for delivering negative messages is, 4 positives to 1 negative:

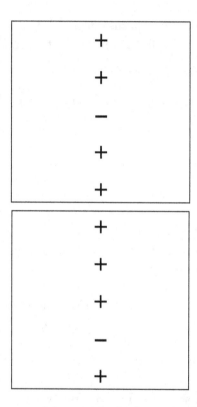

Developing a positive tone in a negative situation:

Always start your correspondence with a positive or at least a very neutral statement. Allow the reader to hear something positive before you bring in the negative. This is sometimes called a "buffer" approach.

Try to use the "sandwich" formula for saying "no"

- Begin with at least two positive or neutral statements

- Place the bad news in the middle

- Try to provide options for the negative messages

- Follow it up with a positive ending

- Try to make your writing action oriented. Emphasize what can be done instead of what can't be done

- Place your emphasis on what's next instead of what's past

- Avoid negative words and emphasize positive words

Words to Avoid

- ✗ Regret
- ✗ Sorry
- ✗ Apologize
- ✗ Unfortunately
- ✗ Can't
- ✗ Won't
- ✗ Couldn't
- ✗ Shouldn't
- ✗ Wouldn't
- ✗ Didn't
- ✗ Don't
- ✗ Fail
- ✗ Never
- ✗ Reject

Words to Emphasize

- ✓ Yes
- ✓ Good
- ✓ Better
- ✓ Best
- ✓ Progress
- ✓ Action
- ✓ Solution
- ✓ Success
- ✓ Excellent
- ✓ New
- ✓ Can & Can do
- ✓ Will
- ✓ Next step
- ✓ Option

✗	Neglect	✓	Alternative
✗	Deny	✓	Choice
✗	Decline	✓	Could
✗	Delay	✓	Would
✗	Trouble	✓	Improved
✗	Problem	✓	Enhanced
✗	Difficulty	✓	Answer
✗	Inconvenience	✓	Assure
✗	But	✓	Positive
✗	Unable	✓	Decision
✗	Unavailable	✓	Approach
✗	Claim	✓	Alternative
✗	Complaint	✓	Resolve
✗	Impossible	✓	Strength
✗	Mandatory	✓	Capacity
✗	Delinquent	✓	Willingness
✗	Penalty		

Here are some examples of the power of positive tone:

Example 1:

Unfortunately, we are unable to attend your board meeting as requested. None of our representatives are available on March 22.

Please accept our apologies and good wishes for a positive meeting.

Rewrite

Thank you for inviting us to your board meeting. We have been looking for an opportunity to address your board.

The date you have chosen is a scheduled all staff meeting for our organization. Do you have any flexibility with your date? One of our representatives could be available on March 21 or 23. Do you have regular monthly meetings? Could you fit us into your April meeting?

Will you call or email to work with us to find a compatible date?

Overall, the best way to ensure your tone stays positive and that you think in terms of the reader is to ask yourself the following questions:

- What can I do?

- What choices can I offer?

- Have I used the "you" attitude?

- What are the alternatives?

- What will happen next?

- Did I use questions?

Develop a Reader Friendly Tone

Business writing has often taken a cold and objective approach. This results in a tone that is bureaucratic and authoritarian. The reader often feels excluded and even, "talked down to."

Words that are used in writing that are not used in conversation, lead the reader to react, instead of taking action. Readers will say, "It's not what he/she said, it's how he/she said it!"

Here are some examples of the reader friendly tone:

Example 1:

It has come to our attention that your monthly report did not arrive as scheduled by March 31. Failure to comply with reporting requirements may result in termination of inclusion in the project.

Rewrite

Did you realize your monthly report was due March 31? Can you confirm when you will complete the report? Inclusion in the project depends on meeting the reporting deadlines. Thank you for sending your report to keep us up to date.

Example 2:

We wish to inform you that your application is currently under review.

You will be advised on the status of your application as soon as a decision is made.

You are requested as a result of this letter to maintain availability for an interview as required in the week of September 19th.

Our best wishes are extended to you as you proceed with the recruitment process.

Rewrite

Thank-you for your application. We are reviewing applications the week of September 12th.

We will update you on your progress by September 17.

Will you be available for an interview the week of September 19? We will call to establish times and location.

Good luck in the recruitment process.

You can create a reader friendly tone by avoiding formal, directive words.

Formal Words	Friendly Words
For your information	Will you review
Please be advised	Did you know
Please comply	Will you. . .
Confirmation required	Will you confirm
We wish to inform	Were you aware
We acknowledge	We received
It is recommended	We recommend
Failure to respond will	You can ensure

It is important to avoid bureaucratic or authoritarian words. Remember that people do not like to be told what to do! They want to discuss and work with you. Again, read your writing aloud. Does it sound like talk?

Chapter 5

Direct Writing—Active and Passive Voice:

One of the best ways to be direct and clear in your writing is to know when to use active and passive writing.

When we were taught writing style and technique, we were often taught to write in the passive style or voice. We often phrased the answer to a question as what was done by whom.

What makes a sentence passive?

Passive   The hammer was carried to the supervisor by John. (Object, Verb, Subject)

In a passive sentence, the subject or doer of the action is secondary to the action, or sometimes not mentioned at all. We know that something is being done, but we may not know who or what did it until the end of the sentence, if at all.

Passive   The report was prepared by the committee. (Object, Verb, Subject)

Passive   The car was driven to the supermarket by myself. (Object, Verb, Subject)

What makes a sentence active?

In an active sentence, somebody or something is doing something. The active style generally phrases the answer to a question as to who / what did what. Is it the simple sentence style.

Active   John carried the hammer to the supervisor. (Subject, Verb, Object)

Active   The committee prepared the report. (Subject, Verb, Object)

Active   I drove the car to the supermarket. (Subject, Verb, Object)

Why is active writing important?

- Uses fewer words

- Emphasizes the people involved

- Leaves fewer questions unanswered

- Sounds less formal

- Is easier to write

- Requires less punctuation

- Is easier to understand

- Is more alive

- Fits with the logical method of reading and thinking

As readers, our logical approach is to read from the active point of view. When we read, we expect to find out who did what. We do not expect to be told what was done by whom. When we come across this sentence order, we are forced to interpret it to match our thought process. Why force your reader to do extra work? Write as much of your information as possible using the active style of writing.

Example:	
Passive:	The instructions were given by the teacher.
Active:	The teacher gave the instructions.
Passive	The decision to expand the department was made by the administrator.
Active	The administrator decided to expand the department.
Passive	An evaluation of the project was done by the safety supervisor.
Active	The safety supervisor evaluated the project.
Passive	The progress of the patient was evaluated by the doctor and the social worker.
Active	The doctor and the social worker evaluated the patient's progress.

Chapter 6

Objective Writing

*I*n order to represent your organization, your department, and yourself effectively, your writing must be factual, specific and objective. It is critical to clearly distinguish between *facts* and *opinions* and between *verifiable* information and *assumptions* and *inferences*. So, what is a fact? A fact is a statement that can be verified, something that can be shown as a certainty. Where do facts come from? You can prove your facts by clarifying them with observations, measurements, precedents, policies, rules, and all of your other senses.

A fact is most clearly stated when it includes the source of the information. Readers are more likely to be influenced by information which is objective and specific.

Example: *I saw two men leave the office at 11:30 a.m.*

This is a statement of fact because it is verified by observation, measurement and accurate word choice. It includes the source for the information.

Example: *Two men were seen leaving the office early this morning.*

This statement is not fact because it is not specific and measurable. The word choice is vague and general. There is no source for the information.

Facts make up the backbone of your writing. Facts stand alone and require less explanation and justification. Opinions may be a part of your writing. However, your opinion should always be supported by fact and clearly labelled as opinion. So, what is an opinion? An opinion is a conclusion that you may believe in implicitly, but it cannot be verified. There is no way to prove an opinion.

An opinion may come as a result of your interpretation of the facts. However, it must clearly be recognized as your opinion.

Example: *I believe the report will be ready by the end of the week.*

This may be a valid opinion, an educated guess or a justified assumption. It may be based on your best information at the time. You may even feel comfortable making this statement. Still, it cannot be proven—it remains to be seen whether or not it is accurate.

The best way to represent your opinions, assumptions, judgements and assessments are by using the following introductory phrases:

→ I believe. . .

→ In my opinion. . .

→ I think. . .

→ It is my opinion. . .

→ My opinion is. . .

These phrases leave no doubt in the reader's mind as to the source of your information. They are clearly opinion statements.

What is *hearsay* information? Hearsay is information, which cannot be verified because the actual source of the information is not available or cannot be disclosed.

Example:

I heard on the bus that a person was killed at the intersection.

This is hearsay because we did not provide a source for the information.

While I was in the restaurant I was told that Faye left for home at 11:30 a.m.

This is hearsay because we don't know where the information originated.

Hearsay information is inappropriate in the writing of any document, which may be viewed by the public.

Factual writing requires specific information. Our traditional writing style has often included vague general statements. Our accountability in the workplace today requires clear, direct language.

Example: *Please send the information requested in the very near future.*

When is the very near future?

Example: *There were several people who expressed interest in a constituency meeting.*

How many are several? Is it enough to warrant scheduling a meeting?

Specific word choice helps us determine positive constructive action.

Example: *The new computer resulted in immeasurable improvements.*

Should we send it back because it didn't improve things enough or should we buy one more to double these results?

On the next page is a list of words and phrases to be aware of as you work to make your writing factual and objective:

Soon	Often
Immediately	Regularly
In the near future	As soon as possible
Temporarily	In the very near future
Few	In a short while
a long period of time	Many
Small amount	an extended stay
Majority	Frequently
On a regular basis	Minority

Chapter 7

The Key Word Concept

*E*very purpose statement should contain a key word or phrase. This key word or phrase will then become a directing force for how you write. The best key words are action words.

Examples:

- Inform
- Convince
- Explain
- Detail
- Recommend
- Show
- Outline

- Persuade
- Describe
- Analyze
- Define
- Conclude
- Demonstrate

Examples:

This report is to persuade you to move to Pacific Plaza.

Persuade is the key word. The rest of your report will concentrate on persuasion. Your approach will be a persuasive one. You will select information to help you in this area. Your summaries and conclusions will be persuasive. In this way, the purpose statement begins directing your report.

This report is to inform you of the progress on project 784.

Again, you have direction for your writing. Information is the key. Your job is to inform your reader. Everything you include in this report must add to the information the reader has. Having this direction will keep you on topic, improve unity and coherence, and allow you to practice economy in your report writing.

Summary

Sometimes, people will ask us to take their research and content and "write it up." This is especially common when people are developing proposals for funding.

We had this experience with an isolated aboriginal community. They were seeking funding for a new recreation centre in their community. The needed funding was extensive and they wanted to write a comprehensive and persuasive proposal.

They sent us their data and we were amazed. The needs analysis was clear and pointed to a greatly needed outcome. They had blueprints, cost analysis, long and short term goals and results. Everything was in order. We went to work developing their proposal.

The end result was a 17 page proposal with a six page appendix. It was a persuasive, convincing document.

The band manager called as soon as he received the proposal. He said, "You can't ask for this much money with only 17 pages of information!" I asked him what he thought he should have? His answer, "A document about 2 ½ inches thick!"

I convinced him, that his information was accurate and it would influence the decision makers as presented. As a result, he asked me to accompany him to the proposal review meetings.

When we arrived, I struggled with my confidence. I saw a pile of proposals in the room. The majority were at least 2 ½ inches thick. I couldn't spot our "little" proposal in the pile of other proposals.

When we were "called in" to discuss our proposal with the panel, I was very nervous. Was I wrong?

As soon as we entered, the lead facilitator put my mind at ease.

"We've granted your proposal," he said. "We've added some contingency to ensure your success." We were speechless! Then he stated, "Yours was the only proposal that we could read and understand, without follow up and further explanation." Then he added, "Congratulations—your community is lucky to have such capable advocates."

What a compliment!

I know that this supports the goals of good business writing.

- The reader only wants to read it once

- The reader wants to be able to understand at the first reading

- The reader wants to be able to make decisions at the first reading

- The reader does not want to have to follow up for clarity and definition

The writer may have to write, rewrite, edit and proof! The reader just wants to read and understand. Write for the reader.